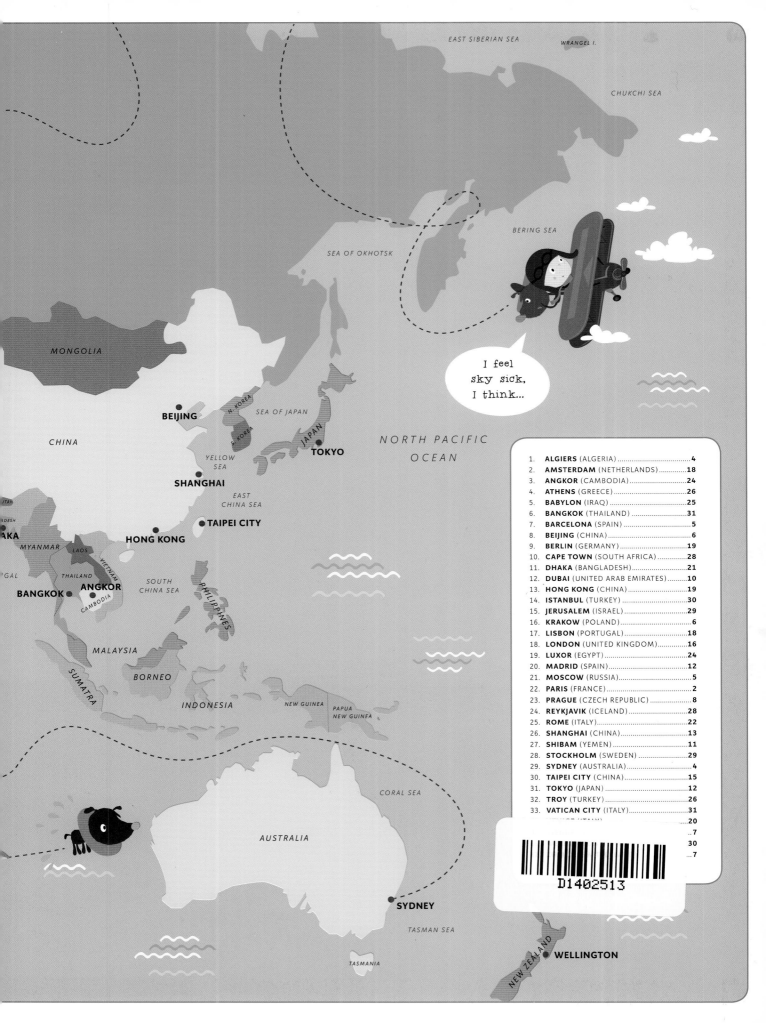

WHO are Bernie and Ben?

TRAVEL THROUGH TOWNS
with Bernie and Ben

HOLLAND

Prague

PARIS

Sydney

Bernie

Come with us!

Ben

Urban Jewels
THE WORLD'S MOST BEAUTIFUL CITIES

They say, "Leave the best for last," but Ben couldn't wait that long. So we put the most beautiful cities right at the beginning. But don't worry, they'll be more fun later on!

PARIS

PARIS IS FRANCE'S LARGEST CITY AND ITS CAPITAL. IT IS ALSO ONE OF THE WORLD'S MOST BEAUTIFUL CITIES. IT LIES ON THE RIVER SEINE AND IS A CENTER OF ART AND FASHION.

BONJOUR!

PARIS is well known for its wide streets, called boulevards. At the end of the **Champs-Élysées**, Paris's most famous boulevard, is the **Arc de Triomphe**. Emperor **Napoleon Bonaparte** built it to honor the soldiers of the Napoleonic Wars.

Hurry up, Ben!

3rd floor

2nd floor

1st floor

Paris's most famous structure, which is visible from all sides, is the **Eiffel Tower**. On its second floor there is a well-known restaurant with a beautiful view of Paris. Don't you agree, Ben?

Eiffel Tower

There are **719** st to the second flo It's too much for me!

Napoleon

Arc de Triomphe

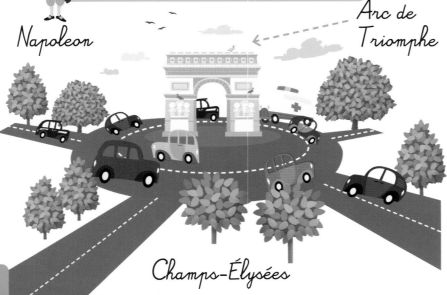

Champs-Élysées

Louvre

In Paris you can go to the world-famous **LOUVRE** Museum. It is one of the biggest art museums in the world.

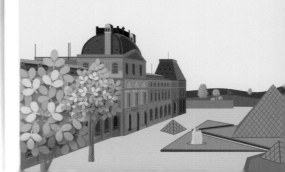

MONTMARTRE

The highest point in Paris is the Montmartre hill. At its top is the beautiful **SACRÉ COEUR** basilica.

Moulin Rouge

The most valuable painting in the Louvre is a famous portrait called the **MONA LISA.**

Beneath Montmartre is the **MOULIN ROUGE** cabaret, where many artists have appeared, including the world-famous singer **Édith Piaf.**

If I don't recognize myself, I'll bite him...

*Very close to the basilica is **Place du Tertre**, a square filled with painters. Ben took advantage of this straight away.*

She has an enigmatic smile. Just like me...

Versailles

Not far from Paris is the beautiful Palace of **VERSAILLES**, where France's royal family lived. It has a magnificent garden full of flower beds and ornamental shrubs.

Mona Lisa

They said I'd look like Louis XIV.

Sydney

SYDNEY is Australia's biggest city. It is located in the hills surrounding **Port Jackson**. Sydney has the world's largest harbor, and one of the most beautiful.

Close to the harbor is Sydney's modern **Opera House**, whose roof looks like a great white sailing ship.

Hold on, Ben!!!

HELP!

There are many beautiful beaches in and around Sydney that are perfect for watersports. We had a great time surfing. Although Ben had a little problem.

Our Lady of Africa

The **OUR LADY OF AFRICA** basilica in Algiers is a magnificent example of French architecture.

ALGIERS

Ketchaoua Mosque

ALGIERS is the largest city and capital city of Algeria in North Africa. It was colonized by the French, whose influence is apparent in the city's architecture. It contains a mixture of African and European elements.

That's a one-humped camel known as a DROMEDARY CAMEL.

Shush!

SALAM ALAIKUM.

The **KETCHAOUA** mosque is a splendid example of the original local architecture. It has beautiful colorful decorations.

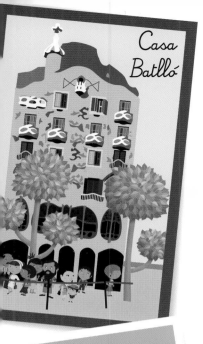

Casa Batlló

BARCELONA is a Spanish city filled with color. The architect **Antoni Gaudí** was instrumental in the creation of its magical appearance.

Antoni Gaudí

Gaudí designed several of Barcelona's most interesting buildings, including **CASA BATLLÓ** and the monumental **SAGRADA FAMÍLIA** church.

Sagrada Família

Gaudí also designed a beautiful Barcelona park. Its entrance is guarded by a lizard with colorful mosaic decoration, like the rest of the park.

The church has been under construction for one hundred years and is still not finished.

Why is it looking at me this way?

MOSCOW is Russia's capital city. It is one of the most beautiful and biggest cities in the world.

ST. BASIL'S CATHEDRAL on Red Square is a symbol of Moscow. It is easy to recognize by its colorful domes.

St. Basil's Cathedral

winter Moscow's temperature can fall to -22°F – so cold that Ben began to speak Russian.

Zdravstvuy mal'chik, ya russkaya sobaka.

In the past only the emperor, his family, and his entourage were allowed to enter the Forbidden City. Those who dared to try were put to death.

Careful, Ben! He looks dangerous.

Forbidden City

BEIJING is the capital city of the People's Republic of China. It used to be the home to Chinese emperors. Inside is the Forbidden City, which was the emperor's palace complex.

Forbidden?

Grrrrr! Grrrrr!

The entrance to the palace is guarded by gilded statues of lions. These statues are often placed in front of important buildings in China.

Forward, march!!!

Wawel

Sukiennice

KRAKOW is one of Poland's most beautiful cities. One of its most popular monuments is **WAWEL CASTLE**. **WAWEL CATHEDRAL** has a crypt where Polish rulers and other important historical figures are buried.

The **SUKIENNICE** is a market building located on Krakow's main square. In the past merchants from all over the world would meet here.

Every year Krakow hosts a festiv[al] procession led by a man dresse[d] as a Tatar on horseback. Know[n] as the **LAJKONIK**, he has beco[me] an unofficial symbol of the cit[y]

Schönbrunn

VIENNA

VIENNA is Austria's capital city and also its biggest. It is known all over the world for its museums, magnificent palaces, coffee houses, and patisseries.

In Vienna we went to explore the splendid Schönbrunn palace. This was the home of the Austrian emperor Franz Joseph and the empress known as Sissi, whose hair was said to reach to the ground.

Hundertwasserhaus

In Vienna you can admire not only wonderful classical architecture but also unique modern buildings, such as the **HUNDERTWASSERHAUS**.

Oh, Ben...

A princess!

Grossmünster

ZURICH

ZURICH is the largest city in Switzerland. It lies on Lake Zurich on the River Limmat and is surrounded by the Alps. One of Zurich's eye-catching buildings is the fascinating **GROSSMÜNSTER** (Great Minster).

ZURICH is the country's financial center and home to most famous Swiss banks.

Phew, was I thirsty!

Zurich has over 12,000 fountains. Most of them have clean water, which Ben happily drank.

PRAGUE

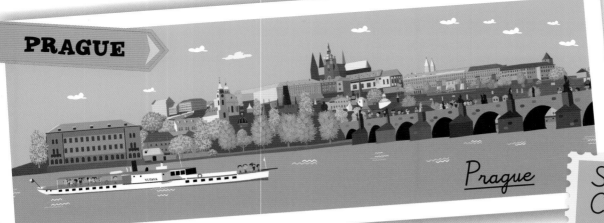

Prague

Prague is often called the "City of One Hundred Spires."

PRAGUE is the capital city of the Czech Republic and a true jewel of central Europe.

> Who wouldn't be, wearing a crown like that?

> Charles IV was a wise and educated monarch.

Charles IV

The towers of **ST. VITUS CATHEDRAL** stand out in the city of Prague. The cathedral is the resting place of important Czech monarchs. Charles IV had a major influence on the cityscape. He ordered the building of the **CHARLES BRIDGE**, a very popular tourist destination.

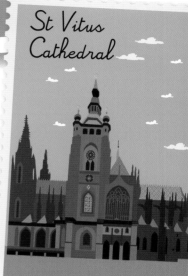

St Vitus Cathedral

LAS VEGAS

All that glitters is not gold.

Ben was thrilled by all the bright lights.

> HELLO!

> Lights! Shows! Fun!

Elvis

LAS VEGAS is in the United States of America. People come from all over for its casinos and shows.

ELVIS PRESLEY, the celebrated king of rock n' roll, can be found all over Vegas. But remember, they're just impersonators.

Urban Giants

CITIES THAT REACH TO THE SKIES

et's not drop the bone!

How do we get down from here?

Ben and I adore skyscrapers. That's why we went to the world's tallest cities.

NEW YORK

NEW YORK CITY

is not only the biggest city in the United States, it is also the biggest in the world. People of all nationalities live here, and it is an important center of world business.

The **STATUE OF LIBERTY**, which is 305 feet tall high, towers over New York Harbor. It was a gift from France as proof of its friendship with the United States.

The most famous part of the city is **MANHATTAN**. It is recognizable by its gigantic buildings and skyscrapers that reach up into the clouds.

King Kong

Empire State Building

Manhattan is dominated by the **EMPIRE STATE BUILDING**, which is 1,454 feet tall. Completed in 1931, it was the world's tallest building for 40 years.

We were right at the top in the statue's headdress. We had an amazing view of the whole city.

Look! It's that big monkey from TV!

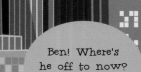

Ben! Where's he off to now? Crazy dog.

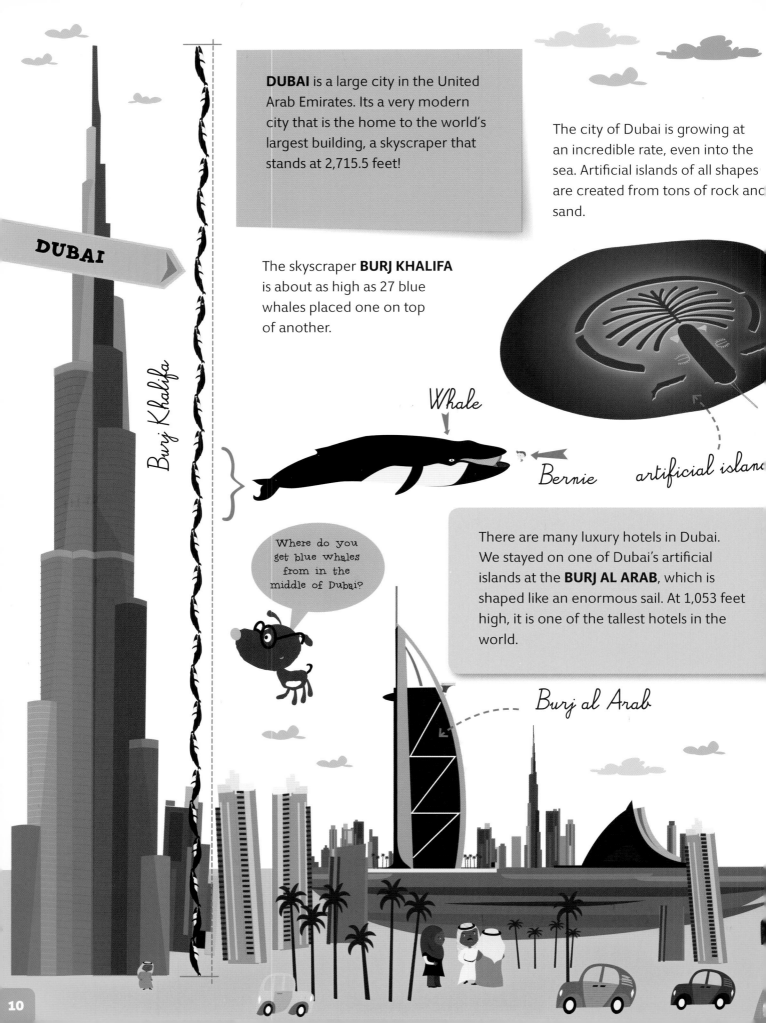

DUBAI

Burj Khalifa

DUBAI is a large city in the United Arab Emirates. Its a very modern city that is the home to the world's largest building, a skyscraper that stands at 2,715.5 feet!

The skyscraper **BURJ KHALIFA** is about as high as 27 blue whales placed one on top of another.

The city of Dubai is growing at an incredible rate, even into the sea. Artificial islands of all shapes are created from tons of rock and sand.

Whale

Bernie

artificial island

Where do you get blue whales from in the middle of Dubai?

There are many luxury hotels in Dubai. We stayed on one of Dubai's artificial islands at the **BURJ AL ARAB**, which is shaped like an enormous sail. At 1,053 feet high, it is one of the tallest hotels in the world.

Burj al Arab

SANTIAGO is the capital city of Chile in South America. It was founded in the 16th century by conquistadors, the Spanish conquerors of the American continent. Here we find Gran Torre Santiago, an unfinished skyscraper that is still taller than any other building in South America.

SANTIAGO DE CHILE

When building a skyscraper, many different factors must be taken into account. For instance, the building must be resistant to earthquakes and high winds.

The majestic peaks of the Andes loom over Santiago. Some of the peaks are taller than 6,000 feet!

When I grow up, I'm going to build skyscrapers.

On our travels from city to city we saw many interesting things. But the desert city of **SHIBAM** was something really special. Shibam is in Yemen, south of the Arabian Peninsula. It consists of high-rise buildings made of mud.

Manhattan of the desert

SHIBAM

Most of these mud "skyscrapers" originated in the 16th century. Because the mud skyscrapers are threatened by rain and erosion, they have to be constantly maintained by the adding of new layers of mud.

Shibam is often called the "Manhattan of the desert".

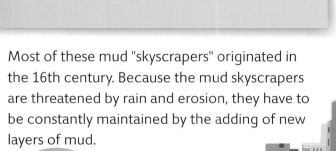

Where to?

Now I'll show how we play soccer...

TAXI

Peep-peep!! Offside!

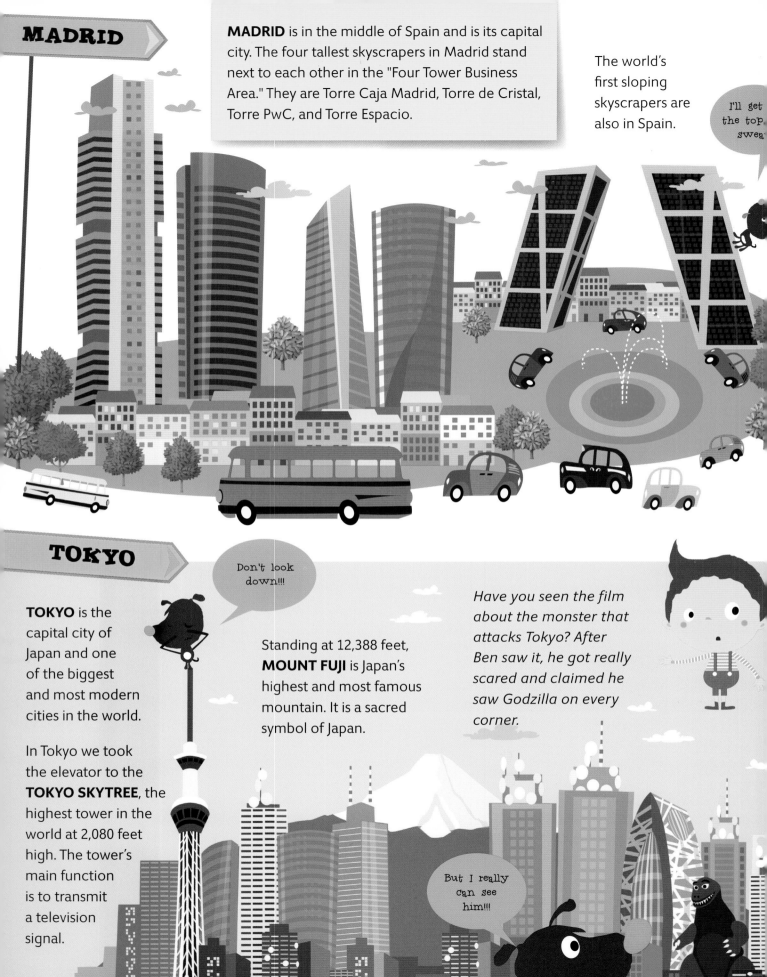

MADRID

MADRID is in the middle of Spain and is its capital city. The four tallest skyscrapers in Madrid stand next to each other in the "Four Tower Business Area." They are Torre Caja Madrid, Torre de Cristal, Torre PwC, and Torre Espacio.

The world's first sloping skyscrapers are also in Spain.

I'll get the top swea

TOKYO

Don't look down!!!

TOKYO is the capital city of Japan and one of the biggest and most modern cities in the world.

In Tokyo we took the elevator to the **TOKYO SKYTREE**, the highest tower in the world at 2,080 feet high. The tower's main function is to transmit a television signal.

Standing at 12,388 feet, **MOUNT FUJI** is Japan's highest and most famous mountain. It is a sacred symbol of Japan.

Have you seen the film about the monster that attacks Tokyo? After Ben saw it, he got really scared and claimed he saw Godzilla on every corner.

But I really can see him!!!

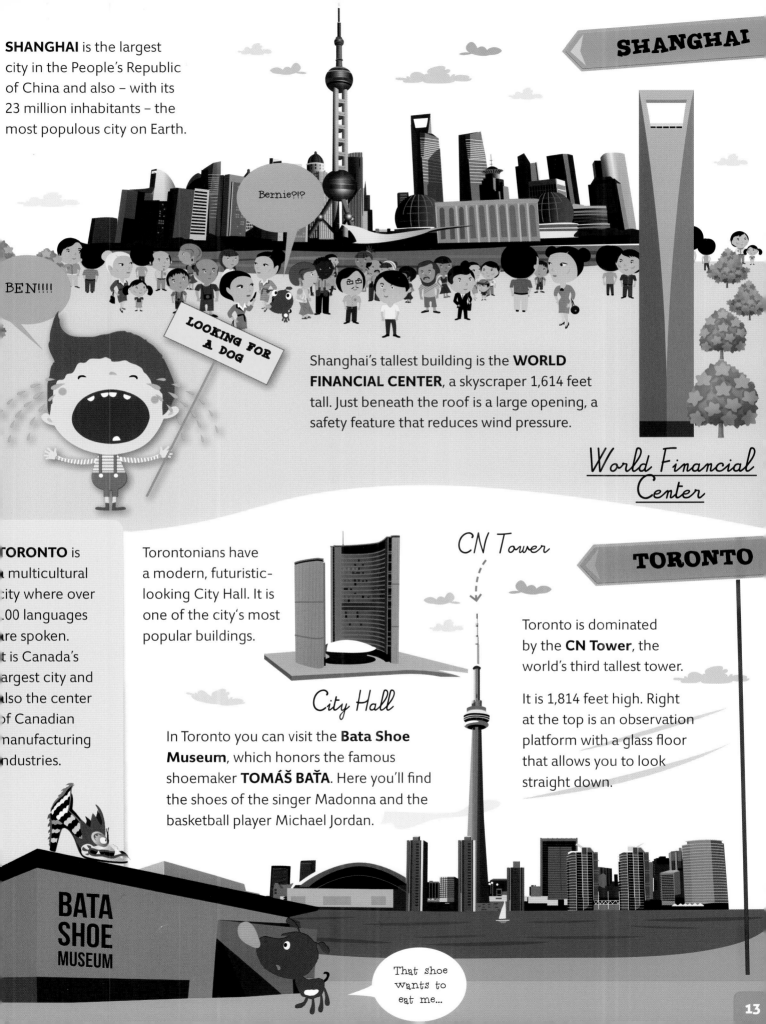

SHANGHAI is the largest city in the People's Republic of China and also – with its 23 million inhabitants – the most populous city on Earth.

SHANGHAI

Bernie?!?

BEN!!!!

LOOKING FOR A DOG

Shanghai's tallest building is the **WORLD FINANCIAL CENTER**, a skyscraper 1,614 feet tall. Just beneath the roof is a large opening, a safety feature that reduces wind pressure.

World Financial Center

TORONTO is a multicultural city where over 100 languages are spoken. It is Canada's largest city and also the center of Canadian manufacturing industries.

Torontonians have a modern, futuristic-looking City Hall. It is one of the city's most popular buildings.

City Hall

CN Tower

TORONTO

Toronto is dominated by the **CN Tower**, the world's third tallest tower.

It is 1,814 feet high. Right at the top is an observation platform with a glass floor that allows you to look straight down.

In Toronto you can visit the **Bata Shoe Museum**, which honors the famous shoemaker **TOMÁŠ BAŤA**. Here you'll find the shoes of the singer Madonna and the basketball player Michael Jordan.

BATA SHOE MUSEUM

That shoe wants to eat me...

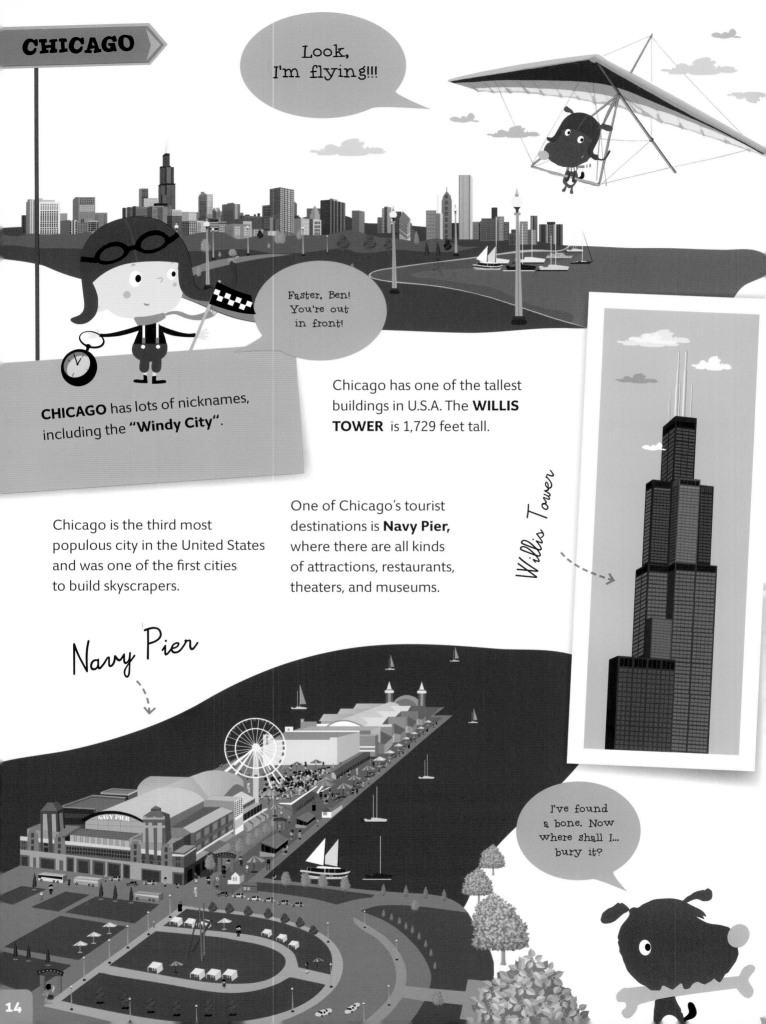

CHICAGO

Look, I'm flying!!!

Faster, Ben! You're out in front!

CHICAGO has lots of nicknames, including the **"Windy City"**.

Chicago has one of the tallest buildings in U.S.A. The **WILLIS TOWER** is 1,729 feet tall.

Willis Tower

Chicago is the third most populous city in the United States and was one of the first cities to build skyscrapers.

One of Chicago's tourist destinations is **Navy Pier,** where there are all kinds of attractions, restaurants, theaters, and museums.

Navy Pier

I've found a bone. Now where shall I... bury it?

TAIPEI CITY is on the island of Taiwan. Its dominating feature is the **TAIPEI 101** skyscraper, which has 101 floors and is 1,671 feet tall.

FITTING ROOMS

In Taipei we even went shopping. The city is famous for its markets that open late. I bought something to wear in one of them...

You look really good in that...

Skyscrapers mostly contain offices, shops, hotels, and private apartments. In the very top stories a space is sometimes reserved for an observatory or a look-out point.

Zooming Around

CITY TRANSPORTATION

The wheel turns so slowly that if we wanted we could hop on.

London Eye

It's really hard work to walk around an enormous city. But Ben and I discovered that there are lots of other ways to travel in a city.

In London there are so many things to see! One of the most famous London buildings is the **PALACE OF WESTMINSTER**, where the United Kingdom's Parliament sits.

Let's go!!!

LONDON

Palace of Westminster

LONDON is the capital of and also the largest city in the United Kingdom of Great Britain and Northern Ireland. It is one of the world's oldest and most magnificent cities.

The British Queen lives in London.

The Queen

TELEPHONE

We traveled around London by subway. There are also places where the **UNDERGROUND** goes above ground. London was the first city in the world to introduce an underground railway system.

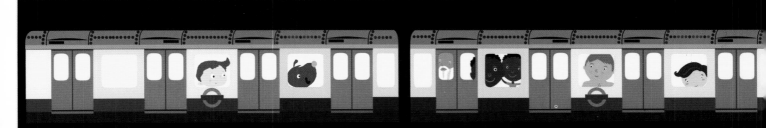

16

The LONDON EYE is Europe's largest Ferris wheel. The Eye has 32 large passenger capsules and one revolution takes about half an hour.

Tower Bridge

small BEN

The River Thames flows through London. The Thames is crossed by **TOWER BRIDGE**, a famous symbol of London. The bridge's construction allows its bascules to be raised when a ship is coming along the Thames into port.

HEATHROW

BIG BEN

One of the towers of the Palace of Westminster is called the **CLOCK TOWER**. Inside this we find the famous great bell called **BIG BEN**, which weighs about 13 tons – about as much as a truck.

BEEFEATER

?!?

We made friends with a Beefeater. It is his job to guard the **TOWER OF LONDON**, one of Her Majesty's palaces and fortresses.

EXCUSE ME.

"Mind the GAP!"

One pound, please.

Toot! Toot!

Double decker

-16-

Red double-decker buses are how many people in London travel. Because of the view from the top deck, they are especially popular with tourists.

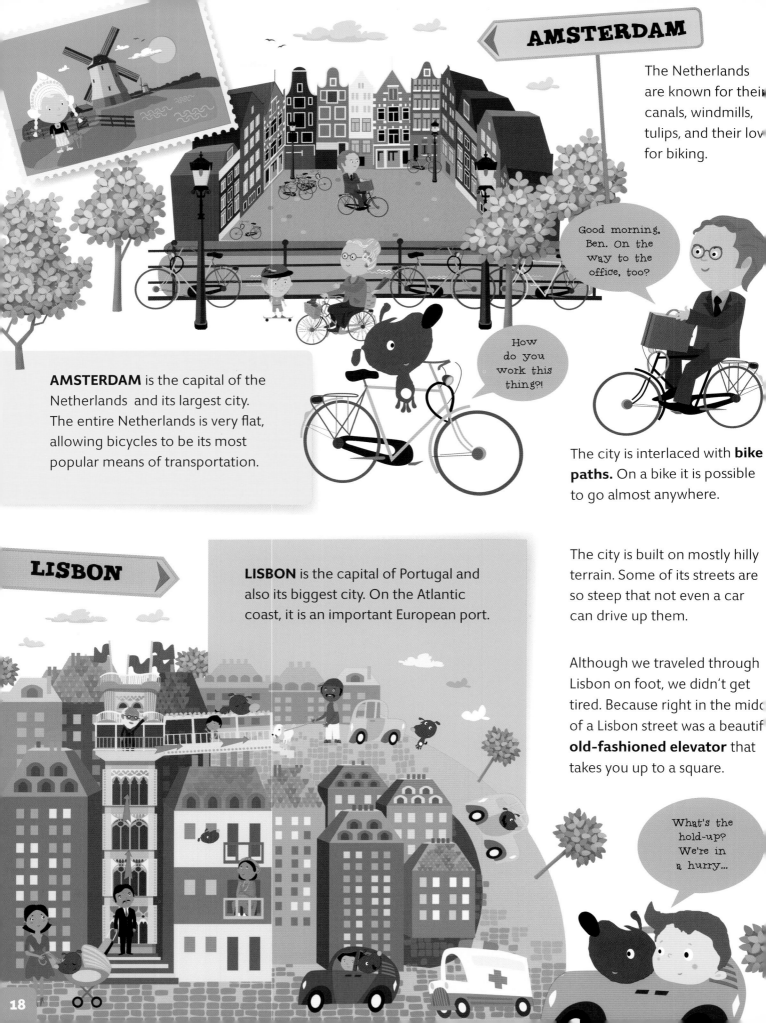

AMSTERDAM

The Netherlands are known for their canals, windmills, tulips, and their love for biking.

> Good morning, Ben. On the way to the office, too?

> How do you work this thing?!

AMSTERDAM is the capital of the Netherlands and its largest city. The entire Netherlands is very flat, allowing bicycles to be its most popular means of transportation.

The city is interlaced with **bike paths.** On a bike it is possible to go almost anywhere.

LISBON

LISBON is the capital of Portugal and also its biggest city. On the Atlantic coast, it is an important European port.

The city is built on mostly hilly terrain. Some of its streets are so steep that not even a car can drive up them.

Although we traveled through Lisbon on foot, we didn't get tired. Because right in the middle of a Lisbon street was a beautiful **old-fashioned elevator** that takes you up to a square.

> What's the hold-up? We're in a hurry...

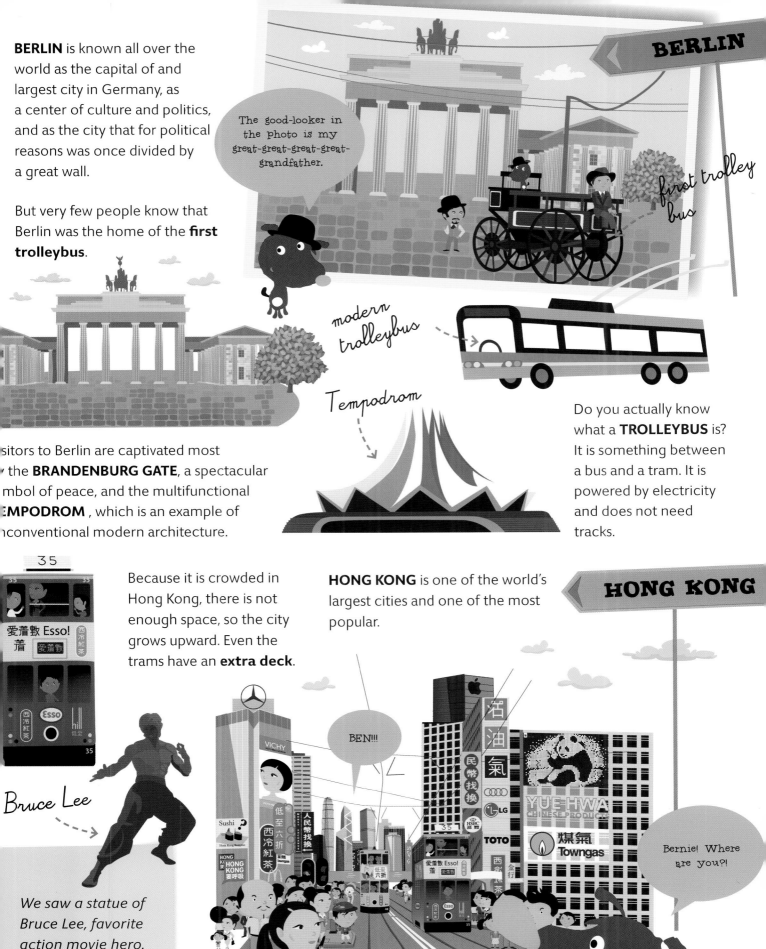

BERLIN is known all over the world as the capital of and largest city in Germany, as a center of culture and politics, and as the city that for political reasons was once divided by a great wall.

But very few people know that Berlin was the home of the **first trolleybus**.

sitors to Berlin are captivated most the **BRANDENBURG GATE**, a spectacular mbol of peace, and the multifunctional EMPODROM , which is an example of nconventional modern architecture.

The good-looker in the photo is my great-great-great-great-grandfather.

first trolley bus

modern trolleybus

Tempodrom

Do you actually know what a **TROLLEYBUS** is? It is something between a bus and a tram. It is powered by electricity and does not need tracks.

Because it is crowded in Hong Kong, there is not enough space, so the city grows upward. Even the trams have an **extra deck**.

HONG KONG is one of the world's largest cities and one of the most popular.

BEN!!!

Bernie! Where are you?!

Bruce Lee

We saw a statue of Bruce Lee, favorite action movie hero.

SAN FRANCISCO

SAN FRANCISCO is the second most populous city in California. It lies between San Francisco Bay and the Pacific Ocean. It is a city of hills and cable cars.

St. Francis
St. Francis
St. Francis
St. Francis

516

"Meet me at the St. Francis"

Golden Gate

Alcatraz

Not far from San Francisco is **ALCATRAZ ISLAND**, where there used to be a famous federal prison for the most dangerous criminals. Al Capone, an American gangster, was an inmate there.

The **GOLDEN GATE** suspension bridge spans the opening of San Francisco Bay. It is painted orange to make it clearly visible to ships even in fog.

VENICE

O-o-o so-o-o-mi-o-o-o...

VENICE is one of the most famous cities in Italy and also the world. Much of Venice is spread across several islands in the Adriatic Sea.

In Venice, instead of streets there are wide canals, where **GONDOLA** boats row along.

Gondolas are traditional Venetian narrow boats. They are all painted black due to an old Venetian law outlawing any other color. There are also special **water buses** in Venice.

DHAKA is Bangladesh's capital and is a large, modern city. It is among the largest and most populous cities in the world. It is referred to as the "Rickshaw Capital of the World," as about 400,000 rickshaws pass through its streets every day.

The **RICKSHAW** is best known in Asia, where it isused like a taxi. There are three types of rickshaws: a (human-powered) pulled rickshaw, a cycle rickshaw, and an auto rickshaw.

Dhaka is also known as the "City of Mosques." Mosques are buildings where Muslims come to worship. The city contains over 700 of them. Dhaka has a tropical climate. Every year it is hit by monsoons that cause heavy flooding.

DHAKA

cycle rickshaw

auto rickshaw

pulled rickshaw

Oof! You've put on weight, Ben!

Faster!

Hi!

Like other coastal cities, Venice is under threat from the constantly rising sea level.

Before Easter, Venice holds a magnificent Carnival where many people wear masks. Venetians make really ingenious masks.

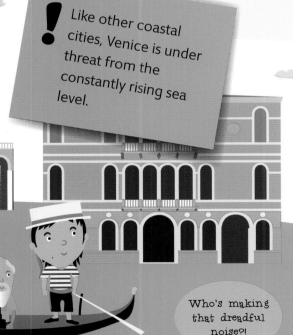

Who's making that dreadful noise?!

Senior Cities
ANCIENT CITIES

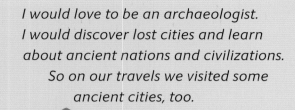

I would love to be an archaeologist. I would discover lost cities and learn about ancient nations and civilizations. So on our travels we visited some ancient cities, too.

Wow...

Julius Caesar

To some extent Rome's appearance was shaped by **Julius Caesar**, the famous Roman statesman and milita leader. For instance, he had t **Circus Maximus** made bigg so that more people could enjoy themselves there.

According to legend Rome was founded by the brothers **Romulus and Remus**, who were raised by a she-wolf.

ROME

Capitoline wolf

They say that all roads lead to Rome. We got there by the first road we took. Ben has never liked ancient monuments, but Rome appealed to him.

Rome is the capital of Italy and historically one of the world's most important cities. It was once the hub of the great Roman Empire, a center of culture, and a place of great events in world history.

And this is how it used to look.

I'm not doing it on purpose. Honestly I'm not.

Many of Rome's monuments are up to 2,500 years old. One of the most amazing is the **Colosseum**. Although construction started in 70 AD, much of it has been preserved.

Colosseum

This is what the Colosseum looks like today.

The Circus Maximus – an oval stadium that was 2,037 feet long – was even more spectacular than the Colosseum. It was the venue for many different cultural and sports events, such as Roman chariot races.

Giddy-up!

Up to 250,000 spectators could fit into the Circus at once.

Today all that remains of the Circus Maximus is its foundations. Where it once stood is now a park that is home to a variety of cultural events.

The best-preserved antique monuments include the **Pantheon**, which was originally built in 27 BC as a pagan temple. But the current Pantheon was built in 126 AD after the first two were burned down.

A circular opening in the Pantheon's dome is the only source of light for the whole interior of the church.

The Colosseum served as a venue for a variety of games and performances. The most popular was gladiatorial combat. Gladiators would fight each other or against lions or bears. The Colosseum had capacity for 50,000 spectators.

M·AGRIPPA·L·F·GOS·TERTIVM·FECIT

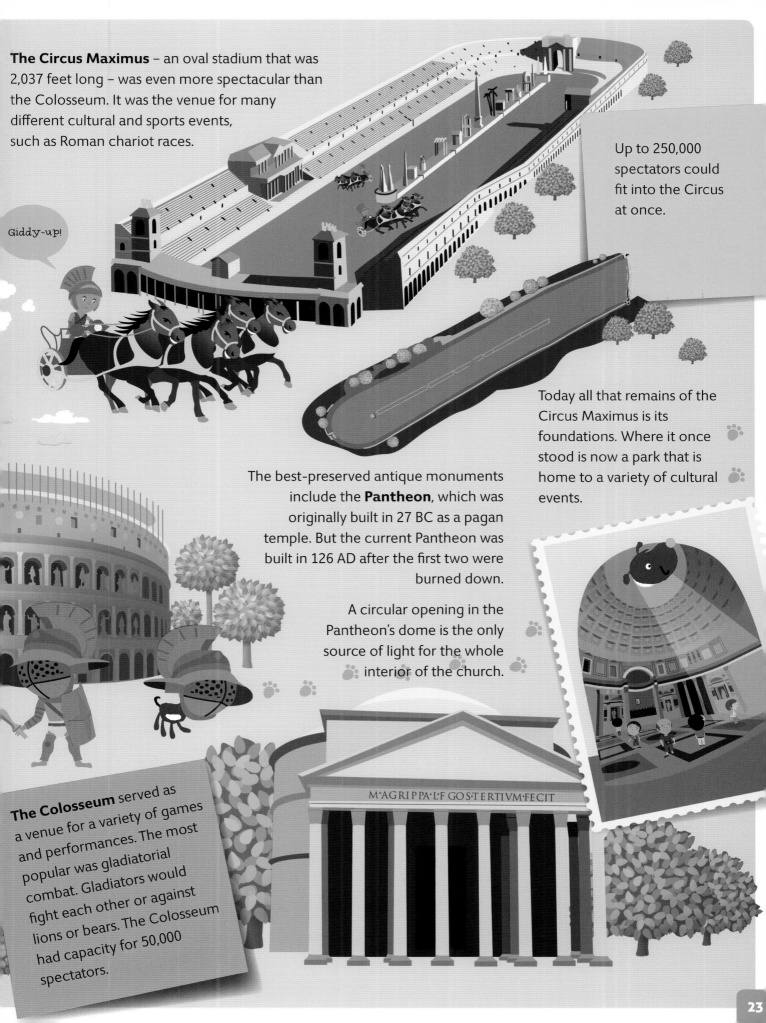

ANGKOR

Angkor is the name of a region in Cambodia. It is located in the well-preserved remains of the huge **Angkor Wat** temple complex.

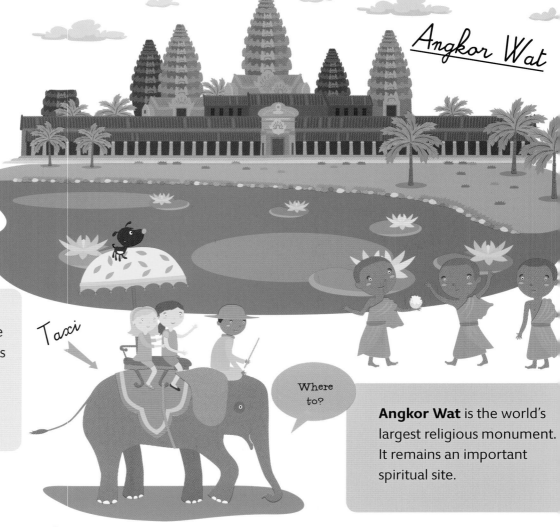

Angkor Wat

The temple was once in the center of one of the world's largest cities, but today it is surrounded by forest wilderness.

Tourists ride into Angkor on a special elephant taxi.

Taxi

Where to?

Angkor Wat is the world's largest religious monument. It remains an important spiritual site.

LUXOR

LUXOR is in Upper Egypt. It is often referred to as "the world's greatest open-air museum." Here we find the remains of the Ancient Egyptian temple complexes of Karnak and Luxor.

We know how the Ancient Egyptians looked from their wall paintings.

?!?

I'm scared. There's bound to be a mummy in there.

Thanks to a computer reconstruction we can figure out what the Luxor Temple looked like. Many beautiful Egyptian paintings and hieroglyphs line the walls.

Luxor used to be called Thebes. It was the capital city of Egypt and seat of the Egyptian god Amun-Ra.

The ancient city of **Babylon** was founded over 4,000 years ago. Its ruins are located in today's Iraq.

There are many legends connected with the city. The most famous of these is the **Tower of Babel**, which was said to reach up to heaven. And it was home to one of the Seven Wonders of the Ancient World, the **Hanging Gardens of Babylon**.

Thanks to archaeologists, restorers, and designers, we can find out how ancient buildings used to look.

The Ishtar Gate

Look! You can see all the way home from here!

One way into Babylon was through the **Ishtar Gate**. It was built with blue-glazed brick.

You can see a copy of the Ishtar Gate in a museum in Berlin.

Tower of Babel

MACHU PICCHU

Machu Picchu was the ancient city of the Incas. We can find its remains in Peru, 7,972 feet above sea level. It was hard work walking up there.

The city was built without the use of mortar or cement. Inca buildings were constructed from perfectly cut blocks that came together like a child's building bricks.

The Incas were the original inhabitants of South America. Their only means of transportation was by llama.

Llama

Inca

That lady or llama??

Don't upset it, Ben, or it'll spit at you.

Other Inca

ATHENS

Athens is the capital of Greece. It spreads over the Attic Peninsula, where the Greeks settled in about 1,900 BC.

The central point of Athens is the **Acropolis** hill, where the **Parthenon** stands.

The Parthenon was a temple for the godde[ss] Athena. Today tourists flock to what remains of it.

Ben! Bernie! Come and study philosophy with us.

Erm-m...

Looking good, eh?

Athens takes its name from **Athena**, the goddess of wisdom. It was a center of education and culture.

Pallas Athena

According to my[...] order to conquer [...] fortified Troy, the G[reeks] resorted to trickery. They [built] a great wooden horse [and] filled it with Greek sol[diers]. They then gave the h[orse] to the Trojans as a [gift]. The Trojans pulle[d the] horse behind the [walls] and into the city. [That] night the G[reek] soldiers jumpe[d out] of the hors[e and] overwhelme[d the] sleepy T[rojans] fo[...]

Today Troy is one o[f] the most famous archaeological site[s] in the world.

TROY

Troy was located where modern-day Turkey currently resides. All that remains of it are ruins, but these help us imagine what it must once have looked like.

The Greek poet **Homer** tells of Troy in his epic works **the Iliad** and **the Odyssey**, which date from around 720 BC. They describe the Trojan Wars and the conquest of Troy by the Greeks.

Trojan horse

Wow... It's a nice trick

Troy

Troy probably looked something like this.

before — now

Unique Cities

We want this book to be interesting right to the end, so now we're going to show you some cities that are truly exceptional.

A symbol of Rio is the 130-feet-high **Christ the Redeemer,** a statue of Jesus Christ that stands on a mountain watching over the city.

Christ the Redeemer

RIO DE JANEIRO

CARNIVAL

Rio de Janeiro is the second biggest city in Brazil and one of the most popular with tourists in South America.

Every year before Lent the huge Rio Carnival takes place. Filled with music and dance, it is one of the biggest and best known carnivals in the world.

The most popular dance at the carnival is **samba**. Dancers decorate floats and wear elaborate costumes to parade through the streets.

Carnival lasts for five days. Ben and I danced the whole way through. We had a marvelous time, even though it was pretty tiring!

Samba de Janeiro!

COOOL!!!

Reykjavik

Reykjavik is the capital and largest city of the island state of Iceland. It is also the northernmost capital city in the world.

Iceland is of volcanic origin. There are a great many **hot springs and geysers** that allow people to indulge in outdoor bathing all year round.

Geysers

I'm not going..

Some of Reykjavik's pavements are heated by hot springs.

CAPE TOWN

Cape Town is the second most populous city in the Republic of South Africa. It is surrounded by many natural beauties, including the amazing Table Mountain that rises majestically over the city.

Near Cape Town there are beautiful, sandy beaches where you can see wild penguins up close.

Ben was rather taken aback by the penguins.

Isn't it too hot for you here?

Penguin

In Cape Town there are people of many cultures and nationalities from over the world

Jerusalem is the capital city of Israel and an important place of pilgrimage and spirituality for three world religions – Christianity, Judaism, and Islam.

Wailing Wall

In Jerusalem we saw a wall that is all that remains of the temple of wise king Solomon. It is known as the **Wailing Wall**. Many people come here to pray.

The Dome of the Rock is one of Jerusalem's most famous sights. The golden dome of this Islamic shrine is impossible to miss.

Gold!

STOCKHOLM

Stockholm is Sweden's capital and largest city. It lies on the mainland and also spreads across 14 islands, which is why it is sometimes known as the "Venice of the North." Its many parts are joined by 57 bridges.

Stockholm is one of the world's cleanest cities. It remains so partly thanks to bicycle transportation, which reduces harmful emissions in the city. The water is so clean that you can fish and bathe right in the center of the city.

In the warmer months it is easy to rent a bicycle in Stockholm.

Venice of the North

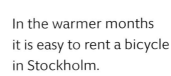

WELLINGTON

Wellington is the capital city of the island state of New Zealand and also the southernmost capital city in the world.

Wellington's original inhabitants were the **Maori**. They wore tattoos that covered their faces.

Maori

Look! Another lizard!

Tuatara

The landscape around Wellington and all over New Zealand is beautiful. There are many animal species here that live nowhere else in the world, such as the tuatara.

ISTANBUL

Istanbul is the largest city in Turkey and – at 3,000 years old – one of the oldest cities in the world. It has an interesting history. It used to be called **Constantinople** and for a time was a capital city of the Roman Empire.

Istanbul is the only city in the world that spreads over two continents. One part lies in Europe, the other in Asia.

The two parts of the city are divided by the **Bosphoru** strait, one of the busiest waterways in the world.

EUROPE

ASIA

And now I'm in Asia.

There's the **Hag Sophia**, a beaut big mosque tha has been made a museum.

Now I'm in Europe.

Bangkok is Thailand's capital and largest city. It is sometimes known as the "Venice of the East" as it lies on a delta and was once interlaced by a network of canals.

Today, too, there are places in Bangkok where people travel by boat. We went to a floating market.

In Bangkok's **Wat Traimit** temple you can admire a golden statue of Buddha. At almost 10 feet high, it is the world's largest golden statue.

Buddha

Pope Francis I.

Very few women live in Vatican City.

Vatican City is a tiny city and state situated in the middle of Rome, Italy. With its 800 or so inhabitants, it is the world's smallest state.

Vatican City is important to the Catholic Church since it is where the Pope resides.

At the center of Vatican City is St. Peter's Square, which is actually round. It is situated in front of St. Peter's Basilica and has space for about 400,000 people.

Do any dogs live there?

31

There are many more interesting cities in the world, but I'm afraid we ran out of time.

The next time you go to a city that you don't know, take a good look around. There are lots of beautiful and amazing things everywhere.

Sorry, we have to fly home now...

Did you enjoy your trip?

AHOOOOOY!

Many Greetings from our Journey!
Yours,
Bernie and Ben

"WHERE WE'VE BEEN!"

And what about our next adventure? Let's have a look to **the PAST!**

THE PAST? GREAT!!

So see you soon!

STERLING CHILDREN'S BOOKS
New York

An Imprint of Sterling Publishing
387 Park Avenue South
New York, NY 10016

Lot #: 10 9 8 7 6 5 4 3 2 1
01/14

STERLING CHILDREN'S BOOKS
and the distinctive Sterling Children's Books logo
are trademarks of Sterling Publishing Co., Inc.

Distributed in Canada by Sterling Publishing,
c/o Canadian Manda Group, 165 Dufferin Street,
Toronto, Ontario, Canada M6K 3H6.

Manufactured in China.
All rights reserved.

www.sterlingpublishing.com/kids

Translated from
TRAVEL THROUGH TOWNS
with Bernie and Ben

Author: Iva Šišperová

Illustrators: Kateřina Hikadová, Zuzana Musilová,
Zuzana Selingerová, Tomáš Tůma, Pavla Kleinová,
Veronika Kopečková

Sterling ISBN 978-1-4549-1238-5

The translation rights arranged
through JNJ Agency.

What
a rush,
guys!

SOUTH PACIFIC
OCEAN